Lerner SPORTS

SPORTS ALL-STARS

DAMIAN LILLARD

Alexander Lowe

Lerner Publications ◆ Minneapolis

SPORTS THRILLS *MEET* RESEARCH SKILLS

Lerner SPORTS

Free Database Trial: **lernersports.com**

Lerner Publications Company
An imprint of Lerner Publishing Group, Inc.
241 First Avenue North
Minneapolis, MN 55401 USA

For reading levels and more information, look up this title at www.lernerbooks.com.

Main body text set in Albany Std. Typeface provided by Agfa.

Library of Congress Cataloging-in-Publication Data

Names: Lowe, Alexander, author.
Title: Damian Lillard / Alexander Lowe.
Description: Minneapolis, MN : Lerner Publications, [2022] | Series: Sports all-stars (Lerner sports) | Includes bibliographical references and index. | Audience: Ages 7–11 | Audience: Grades 2–3 | Summary: "Portland Trail Blazers point guard Damian Lillard is one of the NBA's most exciting scorers. Learn how he became a superstar and see what he does on and off the court to be the best"— Provided by publisher.
Identifiers: LCCN 2021022648 (print) | LCCN 2021022649 (ebook) | ISBN 9781728441153 (library binding) | ISBN 9781728449388 (paperback) | ISBN 9781728445113 (ebook)
Subjects: LCSH: Lillard, Damian, 1990—-Juvenile literature. | Basketball players—United States—Biography—Juvenile literature. | Portland Trail Blazers (Basketball team)—Juvenile literature. | Rap musicians—United States—Biography—Juvenile literature. | Political activists—United States—Biography—Juvenile literature.
Classification: LCC GV865.L52 L69 2022 (print) | LCC GV865.L52 (ebook) | DDC 796.323092 [B]—dc23

LC record available at https://lccn.loc.gov/2021022648
LC ebook record available at https://lccn.loc.gov/2021022649

Manufactured in the United States of America
1-49886-49729-7/15/2021

TABLE OF CONTENTS

DAME TIME

Damian Lillard is a high-scoring point guard and one of the best young basketball players in the world.

- **Date of birth:** July 15, 1990

- **Position:** point guard

- **League:** National Basketball Association (NBA)

- **Professional highlights:** was chosen with the sixth overall pick in the 2012 NBA Draft; is a six-time NBA All-Star; named All-NBA First Team (2018)

- **Personal highlights:** grew up in Oakland, California; has recorded several music albums; has three children

Some of Lillard's greatest games have been against the Oklahoma City Thunder.

The Portland Trail Blazers were matched up against the Oklahoma City Thunder in the first round of the 2019 Western Conference playoffs. Even though the Blazers had a good season, many fans expected the Thunder to win the series. The Thunder had two superstar players in Russell Westbrook and Paul George. But Portland's Damian Lillard refused to go down easily.

The Trail Blazers managed to win three of the first four games, setting them up for a series win. But victory was not guaranteed. The Thunder were too strong. In Game 5, the score was tied 115–115 with only a few seconds left on the clock. It was Dame Time, the part of the game when Lillard takes over. He dribbled the ball near the middle of the court. Instead of driving to the hoop, he pulled up to shoot. The ball swished through the net. The Blazers won the game and the series.

Fans have come to love Lillard for his game-winning shots. He is known for hitting long three-pointers and passing the ball to his teammates for easy baskets. Lillard is one of the most exciting players in the NBA. He has said he wants to play his entire career in Portland and help bring his team an NBA championship. He is truly the face of the Trail Blazers.

FROM OAKLAND
TO UTAH

Lillard is the only former Weber State player currently playing in the NBA.

Damian Lillard was born on July 15, 1990, in Oakland, California.

He worked hard in school and loved to play basketball. He played whenever he had free time.

Lillard was the leading scorer on his college team.

When the outdoor courts were taken over by older players in the summer, Damian didn't leave. He stayed and watched them. He also became very competitive. "I can remember back in seventh grade when I really started to care about when I won or lost and if somebody was better than me," Damian said.

Damian was very small as a kid. As a freshman in high school, he stood only 5 feet 5 inches (1.65 m) tall. He was shorter than most of the top high school players in the US. For his junior and senior years, he attended Oakland High School. He averaged 19 points per game his junior year. But because of his height, he wasn't recruited by big college teams.

In high school in the US, basketball prospects are ranked on a five-star scale. The best players have five stars. Most of the top college teams in the country only want four- and five-star players.

Lillard was the last player at Weber State to wear a number 1 jersey.

Lillard won the Big Sky Conference Player of the Year Award twice.

Damian was a two-star prospect. He signed an offer to attend Weber State University in Utah. Weber State plays in the Big Sky Conference. When Lillard was a freshman, he won the Conference Freshman of the Year Award. He went on to be All-Conference three times and have his number retired by his college. That means no other Weber player will ever wear his jersey number in the future. As he got better at Weber, NBA teams began to notice him.

On June 28, 2012, Lillard was drafted by the Portland Trail Blazers.

At the beginning of Lillard's senior year, many basketball writers did not have him ranked in the top 50 college players in the nation. As the season went on, his ranking rose higher and higher. With one month to go until the 2012 NBA Draft, he was ESPN's eighth-best prospect. So it was a surprise to many when he was taken sixth overall by the Trail Blazers.

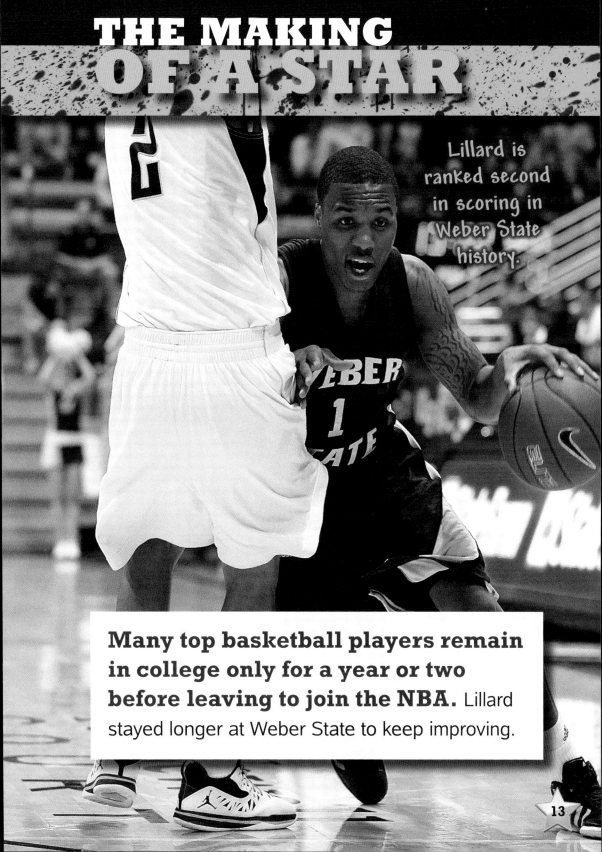

THE MAKING OF A STAR

Lillard is ranked second in scoring in Weber State history.

Many top basketball players remain in college only for a year or two before leaving to join the NBA. Lillard stayed longer at Weber State to keep improving.

Lillard finished his college career as the fifth-ranked scorer in the history of the Big Sky Conference.

But then disaster struck and he nearly did not make it to the NBA. In his junior season, he broke his foot. He had to sit out the rest of the season.

Instead of letting the foot injury stop his progress, Lillard used his time off the court to continue improving. He spent five days a week in the weight room. He studied video of every college game he had played to look for ways to improve. When he returned to the court for his senior season, he was better than he had ever been. That year, he averaged 24.5 points per game. He made an incredible 41 percent of his shots from behind the three-point line.

Watching video of his college games helped Lillard think of ways to play better when he returned from his injury.

Lillard flexes his muscles after scoring a big basket for the Trail Blazers.

Lillard has improved his training even more since he started playing in the NBA. His dedication to working out has made him an NBA star. He uses resistance bands to improve his strength. He puts his muscles through a full range of motions so they are strong moving in every direction. Training his body this way is important to help prevent injuries. It also allows him to play many minutes on the court. In the 2019–2020 season, he led the league by playing 37.5 minutes per game.

For about five months, Lillard was vegan. He didn't eat meat or any products made from animals. In 2018, he started eating meat again. He felt that he was losing too much weight without it. He still eats vegan meals regularly, but he also eats chicken and beef. He says eating a healthful diet has helped him feel more energetic and lighter on his feet during games.

Lillard is one of only two Portland Trail Blazers to play in at least six All-Star Games.

Lillard became interested in rap music while hanging out with his older cousins in Oakland.

Lillard introduces a video featuring rapper Drake at the 2014 ESPY Awards show.

Lillard is not just a basketball player. He is a father, a musician, and a businessperson. Lillard and his partner, Kay'la, have been together since college. In 2018, they had a son, Damian Jr. They had two more kids in 2021, Kalii and Kali.

Lillard endorses shoes and other
Adidas products.

When Lillard became a star in the NBA, he began to endorse products. His biggest deals are with Adidas and Powerade. When he re-signed with Adidas in 2014, it was the third-biggest deal for an NBA player at the time. The only players with bigger deals were LeBron James and Derrick Rose. Adidas believed that Lillard was ready to become a giant superstar.

Getting down to Business

Lillard has several business interests. In 2020, he bought a Toyota car dealership in McMinnville, Oregon. The dealership is called Damian Lillard Toyota, and it has ping-pong tables and special donuts available for customers.

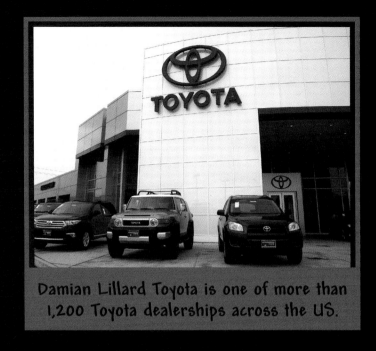

Damian Lillard Toyota is one of more than 1,200 Toyota dealerships across the US.

Lillard also invested in a new Samsung TV Plus channel called PlayersTV. PlayersTV allows athletes to create content and share it directly with their fans. The channel includes shows that give fans a look at different parts of athletes' lives.

Lillard is excited about working with PlayersTV. He says all athletes have unique stories and interests, and PlayersTV allows fans to experience those off-the-court moments.

Lillard did double duty as a player and musical performer at the 2020 NBA All-Star Weekend.

Music fans may know Lillard as rapper Dame D.O.L.L.A. He released his first album in 2016. He has released two more since then. Lillard's rap name stands for Different on Levels the Lord Allows. Lillard is a Christian and brings religious themes to his music.

Lillard is involved in charity work. He partnered with Adidas to build his high school a new gym and weight room. He is also passionate about stopping bullying and helping kids be their best. He started the RESPECT program in 2012. It encourages young people to always show up, work hard, and be kind. "I strive to be the best on the basketball court, but I also work hard to give back to my community and help foster the education of future generations," Lillard said.

In 2020, Black Lives Matter protests took place all around the country. Black Lives Matter's mission is to end violence against Black people. Lillard wanted to use his fame to help promote change. He participated in marches in Portland, Oregon. He helped bring attention to issues that were important to him.

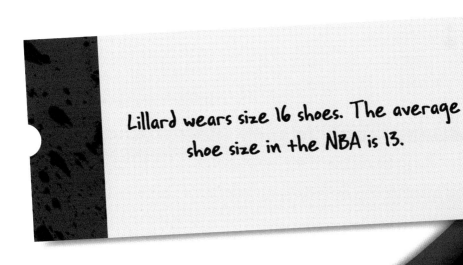

Lillard wears size 16 shoes. The average shoe size in the NBA is 13.

A TRAIL BLAZER FOR LIFE

Lillard has fun warming up on the court before a game.

Lillard wants to play in Portland for his entire career. "Not a lot of guys get to play for one organization for their entire career," he said. "Obviously, I love playing for the Blazers. I love living in the city. I feel like I've established a connection with the people

Rip City is a nickname for Portland. Lillard is a great fit for the team and city.

and the culture of the city just as much as I've done on the basketball court, so that's important." The Trail Blazers haven't won an NBA title since 1977. Lillard wants to be the one to bring a championship back to Portland.

Lillard has finished in the top ten for the Most Valuable Player Award every year since the 2015–2016 season. He has also been All-NBA six times. The league recognizes his greatness, but for Lillard, that isn't enough. He wants to be an NBA champion.

Lillard is one of the best three-point shooters in the NBA.

Lillard set the record for the most three-pointers scored in a player's first two seasons. He is the Trail Blazers' record holder for three-pointers made in a career and is already tenth in NBA history. Within the next few seasons, he will likely climb into the top five.

Lillard plans to continue to use his fame to push for change. He has said that athletes "have to be active participants" in the fight for social justice. Between his success on the court and his achievements off the court, Lillard is an exciting player to follow.

Lillard is one of only three players in history to have 20 points and more than 10 assists in their first NBA game.

All-Star Stats

In just a few seasons with the Trail Blazers, Lillard has proven to be the greatest shooter in team history. He became the team's all-time leader in three-pointers made in just his fourth season. As of June 2021, he had nearly twice as many three-pointers as any other Portland player ever.

Total Three-Pointers Made by Portland Trail Blazers Players

1.	Damian Lillard	2,051
2.	CJ McCollum	1,186
3.	Wesley Matthews	826
4.	Terry Porter	773
5.	Nicolas Batum	751
6.	Damon Stoudamire	717
7.	Clifford Robinson	492
8.	Steve Blake	492
9.	Clyde Drexler	464
10.	Al-Farouq Aminu	417

Glossary

All-Conference: one of the best players in an athletic conference

All-NBA: an award given to the fifteen best NBA players each season

conference: a group of teams that play one another. The NBA has two conferences, the Eastern Conference and the Western Conference.

endorse: to recommend something, such as a product or service, usually in exchange for money

Most Valuable Player Award: an honor given to the best player in the NBA each season

prospect: a player who is likely to succeed at a higher level of play

recruit: to try to secure the services of

resistance band: workout equipment that can be stretched to provide strength training

three-pointer: a shot made from beyond the three-point line

vegan: someone who does not eat meat or products made from animals

Source Notes

9 Candance Bucker, "Blazers' Lillard is just a little kid from Oaktown," *The Columbian*, January 10, 2013, https://www.columbian.com/news/2013/jan/10 /damian-lillard-portland-trailblazers-from-oaktown/.

23 Lindsey Wisniewski, "Trail Blazers guard Damian Lillard teams up with Oakley to give back to his RESPECT Program," *Yahoo! Sports*, March 6, 2021, https://sports.yahoo.com/trail-blazers-guard-damian -lillard-222259335.html.

24–25 Michael Scotto, "'That would be an honor to be a lifetime Blazer': Damian Lillard on his future, CJ McCollum and how to win the West," *The Athletic*, September 6, 2018, https://theathletic. com/508408/2018/09/06/that-would-be-an-honor-to -be-a-lifetime-blazer-damian-lillard-on-his-future-cj -mccollum-and-how-to-win-the-west/.

27 Daniel Roberts, "Damian Lillard on Social Justice: Athletes 'Have to Be Active Participants to Show That This Affects Us Too,'" *Yahoo! Sports*, January 14, 2021, https://www.yahoo.com/lifestyle/damian -lillard-on-social-justice-athletes-have-to-be -active-participants-to-show-that-this-affects-us -too-175531623.html.

Damian Lillard Facts For Kids
https://kids.kiddle.co/Damian_Lillard

Damian Lillard—Portland Trail Blazers
https://www.nba.com/player/203081/damian_lillard

Flynn, Brendan. *Portland Trail Blazers All-Time Greats (NBA All-Time Greats)*. Mankato, MN: Press Box Books, 2020.

Levit, Joe. *Basketball's G.O.A.T.: Michael Jordan, LeBron James, and More*. Minneapolis: Lerner Publications, 2020.

Monson, James. *Behind the Scenes Basketball*. Minneapolis: Lerner Publications, 2020.

Portland Trailblazer's Damian Lillard: Q&A With the NBA Rookie Of the Year
https://www.sikids.com/hoop-head/damian-lillard

Index

Photo Acknowledgments

Al Bello/Staff/Getty Images, p.4; Steve Dykes/Stringer/Getty Images, p.6; Chris Williams/Icon SMI/Newscom, p.8; Boyd Ivey/Icon SMI/Newscom, p.9; Boyd Ivey/ Icon SMI/Newscom, p.10; Mark Halmas/Icon SMI/Newscom, p.12; Thurman James/ Cal Sport Media/Newscom, p.13; Boyd Ivey/Icon SMI/Newscom, p.14; Chris Williams/ Icon SMI/Newscom, p.15; Abbie Parr / Stringer/Getty Images, p.16; Gabe Ginsberg/ Stringer/Getty Images, p.18; Kevin Winter/Staff/Getty Images, p.19; Imaginechina Limited/Alamy, p.20; Justin Sullivan / Staff/Getty Images, p.21; Jonathan Daniel / Staff/Getty Images, p.22; Steph Chambers / Staff/Getty Images, p.24; Abbie Parr / Stringer/Getty Images, p.25; Abbie Parr / Stringer/Getty Images, p.26; Melissa Sue Gerrits/Getty Images, p.27

Cover: EzraShaw/Staff/Getty Images